PIRATES

VS.

NINJAS

Disclaimer:
The battles in this book are not real. It is fun to imagine. These 2 opponents would never fight each other in real life.

⬤ 45th Parallel Press

Published in the United States of America by Cherry Lake Publishing
Ann Arbor, Michigan
www.cherrylakepublishing.com

Reading Adviser: Marla Conn, MS, Ed., Literacy specialist, Read-Ability, Inc.
Book Designer: Melinda Millward

Photo Credits: © metamorworks/Shutterstock.com, back cover, 12, 16; © FoodAndPhoto/Shutterstock.com,
cover, 5; ©Iain Masterton/Alamy Stock Photo, cover, 5; © katalinks/Shutterstock.com, 6; © Tithi Luadthong/
Shutterstock.com, 9; © peepo/istock, 10; © Nikola Knezevic/Shutterstock.com, 15; © GraphicsRF/Shutterstock.
com, 19, 20; © Digital Storm/Shutterstock.com, 19; © vectortatu/Shutterstock.com, 20; © Guayo Fuentes/Shut-
terstock.com, 21; © Katiekk/Shutterstock.com, 23; © Sergei Mokhov/Shutterstock.com, 24; © Jim Lambert/
Shutterstock.com, 25; © LookerStudio/Shutterstock.com, 25; © Fernando Cortes/Shutterstock.com, 27;
© Fer Gregory/Shutterstock.com, 29

Graphic Element Credits: © studiostoks/Shutterstock.com, back cover, multiple interior pages; © infostocker/
Shutterstock.com, back cover, multiple interior pages; © mxbfilms/Shutterstock.com, front cover; © MF
production/Shutterstock.com, front cover, multiple interior pages; © AldanNi/Shutterstock.com, front cover,
multiple interior pages; © Andrii Symonenko/Shutterstock.com, front cover, multiple interior pages; © acidmit/
Shutterstock.com, front cover, multiple interior pages; © manop/Shutterstock.com, multiple interior pages; ©
Lina Kalina/Shutterstock.com, multiple interior pages; © mejorana/Shutterstock.com, multiple interior pages;
© NoraVector/Shutterstock.com, multiple interior pages; © Smirnov Viacheslav/Shutterstock.com, multiple
interior pages; © Piotr Urakau/Shutterstock.com, multiple interior pages; © IMOGI graphics/Shutterstock.com,
multiple interior pages; © jirawat phueksriphan/Shutterstock.com, multiple interior pages

Copyright © 2020 by Cherry Lake Publishing

All rights reserved. No part of this book may be reproduced or utilized
in any form or by any means without written permission from the publisher.

45th Parallel Press is an imprint of Cherry Lake Publishing.

Library of Congress Cataloging-in-Publication Data

Names: Loh-Hagan, Virginia, author.
Title: Pirates vs. ninjas / by Virginia Loh-Hagan.
Other titles: Pirates versus ninjas
Description: [Ann Arbor] : [Cherry Lake Publishing], [2019] | Series: Battle royale : Lethal warriors | Audience:
    Grades: 4 to 6. | Includes bibliographical references and index.
Identifiers: LCCN 2019003645| ISBN 9781534147645 (hardcover) | ISBN 9781534150508 (pbk.) | ISBN
    9781534149076 (pdf) | ISBN 9781534151932 (hosted ebook)
Subjects: LCSH: Pirates–Juvenile literature. | Ninja–Juvenile literature.
Classification: LCC G535 .L624 2019 | DDC 910.4/5–dc23
LC record available at https://lccn.loc.gov/2019003645

Printed in the United States of America
Corporate Graphics

About the Author

Dr. Virginia Loh-Hagan is an author, university professor, former classroom teacher,
and curriculum designer. She likes to think she's a ninja. But she's too loud. She
lives in San Diego with her very tall husband and very naughty dogs. To learn more
about her, visit www.virginialoh.com.

Table of Contents

Introduction

Imagine a battle between pirates and ninjas. Who would win? Who would lose?

Enter the world of *Battle Royale: Lethal* **Warriors**! Warriors are fighters. This is a fight to the death! The last team standing is the **victor**! Victors are winners. They get to live.

Opponents are fighters who compete against each other. They challenge each other. They fight with everything they've got. They use weapons. They use their special skills. They use their powers.

They're not fighting for prizes. They're not fighting for honor. They're not fighting for their countries. They're fighting for their lives. Victory is their only option.

Let the games begin!

In real life,
nobody really
wins in a war.

PIRATES

Some pirates were part of the slave trade.

Pirates were robbers of the sea. They were sailors. They attacked, **seized**, and destroyed ships. Seize means to take over control. Pirates did this to ships at sea. They did this to ships docked on land.

Pirates **looted**. Loot means to raid and steal. Pirates **smuggled**. Smuggle means to secretly move things. They moved things in and out of countries. Smuggling is against the law. Pirates were **criminals**. Criminals are people who break laws. If caught, pirates were punished with death.

Pirates stole for money. Some pirates liked taking risks. They liked living dangerous lives. They were hungry for adventures. They liked the freedom of the seas.

Some pirates became famous. These pirates made piracy seem fun. But life at sea was tough. Pirates didn't live very long. They led violent lives. Sometimes they got captured. Or they died in a sea storm. Or they died in a battle.

Pirates attacked all kinds of ships. They didn't care where the ships came from. They attacked shipping lanes. They messed up trade routes. Pirate ships had many guns. Pirates fought with guns, swords, and knives. They also fought with small shields. They got on board ships. They attacked. They killed people to steal their **cargo**. Cargo is supplies. When done stealing, pirates sank ships.

Pirates called certain areas "hunting grounds."

People feared pirates. When pirates saw ships, they raised pirate flags. They fired **cannons**. Cannons are large gun machines. Pirates warned the other ship. Most people **surrendered**. Surrender means to give up. These people didn't fight back. They let pirates take their stuff. But some people fought back. That was their mistake. Pirates were tough fighters.

Pirates took prisoners. They also punished pirates who acted up. They sold people as slaves. They made people walk the plank. They left people on islands. They whipped people. They **keelhauled** people. Keelhauling meant death for someone. Pirates tied people up. They threw them overboard. They dragged people under the ship.

FUN FACTS ABOUT PIRATES

- Ching Shih lived from 1775 to 1844. She was a Chinese pirate queen. She attacked the China seas. She commanded up to 1,800 ships. She may have had 40,000 pirates under her control. She's the most successful pirate. She had the largest crew ever.

- There were many pirates in the Caribbean Sea. Pirates needed to hide. The Caribbean has many islands. It has many bays. It has a lot of hiding spots. Pirates could hide from the law. They could also hide their treasure.

- The golden age of pirates was approximately from 1650 to 1725. Several factors made this so. First, many young men were out of work. They needed jobs. Second, there were many shipping lanes. People were exploring lands. They had ships full of things. Third, there were little or no laws. Great Britain wanted to stop piracy. Royal Navy ships fought against pirates. Pirate hunters were sent.

- September 19 is International Talk Like a Pirate Day. People should talk in "maritime pidgin English." They say things like "Ahoy, maties!"

NINJAS

Ninjas did sneaky work.
This made them dishonorable.

Ninjas came from Japan. They were mainly from Iga and Koga. These are Japanese villages. The Iga and Koga **clans** created ninjas. Clans are families. Iga and Koga were deep in the mountains. They were hidden away from other people. Most ninjas were from the lower classes. They were workers. Nobody paid attention to them. This was good for ninjas.

Ninjas were top secret agents. They were spies. They were killers. They were hired by rich people. They found out secrets. They tricked people. They traded their services for money. They did this without honor or glory. This meant they were **outlaws**. Outlaws are people who break the law.

Ninjas trained. They went to ninja schools. They learned **ninjutsu**. Ninjutsu is a fighting style. Ninjas learned fighting skills. They learned **stealth**. Stealth means to move quietly. Ninjas learned to **camouflage**. Camouflage means to blend in. Ninjas learned to **sabotage**. Sabotage means to mess things up on purpose. Ninjas learned ways to escape. They learned to use ropes to climb. They learned survival skills. They learned to heal themselves.

Ninjas tricked people. They didn't want enemies to know they were there. They wore disguises. They wore black. They snuck into places. They made traps. They hid weapons. They got information. They used this info to kill or sabotage. They hit and ran. They're known for sneak attacks.

Ninjas learned to observe their surroundings.

Ninjas used a lot of weapons. They mainly used weapons to distract. They set things on fire. They set off bombs. They threw darts. They used powder.

They used weapons to kill. They used swords called **katanas**. They used bows and arrows. They used spears. They used **nunchucks**. Nunchucks are sticks on a chain. Ninjas used normal objects as weapons. Examples are sharp hairpins or pens. Ninjas dipped their weapons in poison.

There were many stories about ninjas. These stories made ninjas sound scarier. People thought ninjas could walk on water. They thought ninjas could fly. They thought ninjas had magic. They thought ninjas could change shapes. They thought ninjas were **invisible**. Invisible is not being seen.

FUN FACTS ABOUT NINJAS

- Iga-Ueno is a city in Japan. It celebrates its ninja history. The city hosts a ninja festival every year. It lasts 5 weeks. It's from early April to May 5. People dress up as ninjas. They act out ninja attacks.

- Some ninjas stole their enemies' paper lanterns. These lanterns had the enemies' signs. Ninjas made copies of these lanterns. They walked into their enemies' castles. They set the castles on fire. Then, they escaped.

- Ishikawa Goemon lived from 1558 to 1594. He was a ninja hero. There are many stories about him. People believed that he stole from the rich to give to the poor. Goemon and his son tried to kill a bad ruler. They were caught. They were punished. They were boiled alive.

- Ninjas passed secret messages. They created special systems. For example, they used colored rice. Each rice color had different meanings.

- Ninjas used cats to tell time. They looked into a cat's eyes. Cat's eyes are sensitive to light. Their eyes change shape during the day.

CHOOSE YOUR BATTLEGROUND

Pirates and ninjas are fierce fighters. They're well-matched. They're both free from laws. They fight for themselves. But they have different ways of fighting. So, choose your battleground carefully!

Battleground #1: Sea

• Pirates are masters at sea. They're expert sailors. They know a lot about ships. They also have powerful warships with lots of guns. They work well together on ships. They follow their captain's orders. They do their jobs.

• Ninjas fight on land more. But they do live on an island. Islands are surrounded by water. Ninjas might not be able to sail. But they're trained to fight anywhere. So, they'd be able to fight on ships. They can also hold their breath underwater.

Pirates may travel as a fleet.
Fleets are groups of ships.

Battleground #2: Land

- Pirates like the sea because they can escape faster. But they do go to land. They spend their money there. They like to party. But they're always ready to fight. They might not be as well-organized on land.

  - Ninjas can fight on land. There are lots of places for them to hide.

Battleground #3: Mountains

- Pirates don't spend much time on mountains. The mountains are too far from the sea. Pirates are used to warmer weather. They won't know their way around.

- Ninjas were trained on mountains. They'd have no problem fighting on mountains. They're good climbers. They climb a lot of walls. They know how to use ropes and other tools.

ARMED AND DANGEROUS: WEAPONS

Pirates: Pirates are famous for using cutlass swords. Cutlass swords have one sharp cutting edge. Their blades are a little curved. Cutlass swords weigh 3 pounds (1.4 kilograms). They're 2 feet (61 centimeters) long. They're short enough to fight in close combat. They're good for fighting on decks or below deck. They're long enough to slash. They can easily break down wood doors. They can tear cloth. They can cut ropes. They're mainly used on ships.

Ninjas: Ninjas use shuriken. Shuriken means "hand hidden blades." They're hidden weapons. They're used for throwing and stabbing. They're small. They're sharp. They're made from everyday things. Examples are nails, knives, and metal. Shuriken were used with main weapons. Main weapons are swords or spears. Shuriken were used to distract. They're known as "ninja stars." The star is one of many shapes shuriken can take. Shuriken can also be spikes. They're ninja's secret weapons.

FIGHT ON!

The battle begins. Rich men need to ship their gold. They're worried about pirates. They hired ninjas to protect their ship. Pirates spot the ship. They want to loot the ship. They don't see any guards on board. They yell out, "Surrender or die!" The ship refuses. They continue to sail on.

Move 1:

Pirates use **grappling hooks**. Grappling hooks can be fired from special cannons. They are large hooks attached to heavy line. Pirates shoot out the hooks at the ship. The hooks take hold. They attach to the wood and sails. Pirates reel in the ship. They pull the ship close to them. Then, they get on the other ship.

Some pirates trick victims. They pretend to need help. Then, they attack.

Move 2:

Ninjas throw eggshells at the pirates. The eggshells break. They're smoke bombs. Pirates cough. They wipe their eyes. They can't see or move. A group of ninjas sneaks on board the pirate ship. They make traps. They leave poisoned coins everywhere. If pirates pick them up, they'll die. Ninjas steal the pirates' weapons.

Move 3:

Pirates from the back move to the front. They're not as affected by smoke. They wave their swords and guns. They slash and shoot anything in their way. Pirates on the ship shoot cannons. They shoot everywhere. They board the ship from different directions. Time is important. The faster they take over, the less time the ninjas can fight. Pirates move quickly.

Ninjas use spears in battle.
Spears have a long range.

LIFE SOURCE: FOOD FOR BATTLE

Pirates: Pirates ate salted or dried beef. The meat looked like black wood. Pirates drank a lot of beer. Since they were at sea, it was hard to get fresh water. Beer was the safest thing to drink. Pirates mainly ate hardtack. Hardtack is a type of bread. It's also called ship's biscuit. It looks like a cracker. It's made of flour, water, and salt. It's cheap. It lasts a long time.

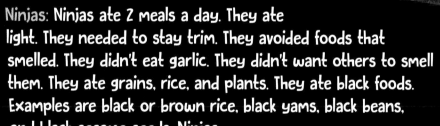

Ninjas: Ninjas ate 2 meals a day. They ate light. They needed to stay trim. They avoided foods that smelled. They didn't eat garlic. They didn't want others to smell them. They ate grains, rice, and plants. They ate black foods. Examples are black or brown rice, black yams, black beans, and black sesame seeds. Ninjas thought black food warmed their bodies. They thought it made them more active. They thought it was healthier.

Move 4:

Ninjas climb on the ship's walls and **masts**. Masts are tall poles that hold up sails. Ninjas throw small blades at pirates. They aim for eyes. They aim for hands. Then, they use their spears to stab. They run away.

Move 5:

A group of pirates get out of the main fighting area. They get into small boats. They circle around the ninjas' ship. They shoot a lot of bullets. They aim for anything that moves.

Move 6:

Ninjas make a sticky bomb of red pepper dust. They throw it at pirates. They take out their katanas. They stab the bombs. The spicy dust explodes. It flies into the pirates' eyes. It also burns any stab wounds.

Wooden legs and eye patches are
often associated with pirates.

AND THE VICTOR IS . . .

What are their next moves?
Who do you think would win?

Pirates could win if:

- They outsmart ninjas. They need to figure out ninjas' secret weapons and tricks. Ninjas are good at distracting their enemies.

- They keep their plans secret. Remember, ninjas are spies. They're always listening. They like to be one step ahead.

- They get ninjas to fight. Ninjas would rather hide than fight.

Ninjas could win if:

- They don't let pirates break down their spirits. Pirates are loud. They like to brag. They make threats.
- They get pirates out of the sea. They're good sailors. They're at their best on ships.
- They separate pirates from their captains. Pirates don't work as well without their leader.

Both pirates and ninjas work for money. They could be bribed.

Pirates: Top Champion

Blackbeard was the most feared pirate. He had a thick black beard. He carried many weapons across his chest. His real name might have been Edward Thatch. He worked for Great Britain. He captured a French slave ship. He turned it into his warship. He added 40 guns. He called it *Queen Anne's Revenge*. He attacked ships along the Virginia and Carolina coasts. He also attacked the Caribbean Sea. In 1718, he based himself in North Carolina. He forced people to pay him. He looted towns. People in North Carolina had enough of Blackbeard. They asked the British navy for help. The British navy fought Blackbeard. Blackbeard was stabbed 20 times. He had five gunshot wounds. The British put his head on top of their ship. Blackbeard is famous for burying treasure. His treasure has never been found. His ship was found by divers in the 1990s.

Ninjas: Top Champion

Mochizuki Chiyome was a Japanese poet. She was a rich noble. Noble means she's from a high class. Chiyome was from the Koga clan. She became a female ninja. She led a kunoichi. Kunoichi is a group of female ninjas. Chiyome recruited many girls. She recruited orphans, refugees, and slaves. Orphans are people who lost their parents. Refugees are people who escape from dangerous countries. Slaves are people who are owned by other people. People thought Chiyome was giving these girls a better life. But, in fact, Chiyome was training the girls in secret. She trained 200 to 300 girls. Her kunoichi disguised themselves. They dressed as traveling medicine women. They dressed as actresses. They worked as servants. They worked as maids. They moved from town to town. They got inside castles. They spied on warlords. They gathered information for the Takeda clan. Takeda was Chiyome's husband's uncle. She disappeared from record in 1573.

Consider This!

THINK ABOUT IT!

- How are the pirates and ninjas alike? How are they different? Are they more alike or different? Why do you think so?
- If the pirates and ninjas lived at the same time, do you think they would've fought each other? If they did, who would've won? Why do you think so?
- Think about your skills. What skills would make you a good pirate? What skills would make you a good ninja? Would you rather be a pirate or ninja? Explain why.
- What's the difference between a pirate and privateer? How are they alike? How are they different?
- Learn more about samurai warriors. Compare them to ninjas. How are they alike? How are they different?
- Compare pirates in history to today's pirates. How have pirates changed over time? How have they stayed the same? What are the risks and benefits of being a pirate?

LEARN MORE!

- Bunting, Eve, and John Manders (illust.). *P Is for Pirate: A Pirate Alphabet*. Ann Arbor, MI: Sleeping Bear Press, 2014.
- Krull, Kathleen, and Kathryn Hewitt (illust.). *Lives of the Pirates: Swashbucklers, Scoundrels*. Boston, MA: Harcourt Children's Books, 2010.
- Lee, Adrienne. *Ninja*. North Mankato, MN: Capstone Press, 2014.
- Osborne, Mary Pope, Natalie Pope Boyce, and Sal Murdocca (illust.). *Ninjas and Samurai: A Nonfiction Companion to Magic Treehouse #5: Night of the Ninjas*. New York, NY: Random House, 2014.

GLOSSARY

camouflage (KAM-uh-flahzh) to blend into one's surroundings

cannons (KAN-uhnz) heavy gun machines mounted on wheels

cargo (KAHR-go) supplies or goods carried on ships, planes, or cars

clans (KLANZ) families

criminals (KRIM-uh-nuhlz) people who break the law by committing crimes

grappling hooks (GRAP-ling HUKS) large hooks connected to heavy lines that can be fired from ships

invisible (in-VIZ-uh-buhl) not able to be seen

island (EYE-luhnd) land surrounded by water

katanas (kuh-TAHN-unz) long, single-edged swords used by Japanese warriors

keelhauled (KEEL-hawld) to tie and drag a person under a boat

looted (LOOT-id) raided and robbed

masts (MASTS) tall poles that hold up sails on a ship

ninjutsu (nin-JUT-soo) a fighting style focused on stealth, camouflage, and sabotage

nunchucks (NAHN-chuks) two sticks connected by a chain used as a weapon

opponents (uh-POH-nuhnts) fighters who compete against each other

outlaws (OUT-lawz) people who have broken the laws

sabotage (SAB-uh-tahzh) to mess things up on purpose

seized (SEEZD) took over control

smuggled (SMUHG-uhld) to illegally move things in and out of a country

stealth (STELTH) to move quickly and quietly without being seen

surrendered (suh-REN-durd) quit

victor (VIK-tur) the winner

warriors (WOR-ee-urz) fighters

INDEX